Informing the legislative debate since 1914

Securing U.S. Diplomatic Facilities and Personnel Abroad: Legislative and Executive Branch Initiatives

Analyst in Foreign Affairs

February 3, 2014

Congressional Research Service
7-5700
www.crs.gov
R43195

Summary

The September 11, 2012, attack on U.S. facilities in Benghazi, Libya, prompted sustained congressional attention on the specific circumstances of the events in question, as well as broader questions regarding how U.S. diplomatic personnel and facilities abroad are secured. Ensuring that the Department of State is better prepared for the possibility of similar attacks in the future has been a central congressional concern.

The Department of State undertook a number of measures in response to the attack, including immediate steps to bolster security at posts around the world; an investigation of the incident through an Accountability Review Board; and longer-term measures implementing the board's recommendations, including requests for significantly greater funding than in recent years.

Congress has conducted oversight through investigations by a number of committees and through a number of hearings. Members have also put forward legislative proposals on issues ranging from the composition of Accountability Review Boards to procedures for awarding local security guard force contracts.

In the 113th Congress, two wide-ranging bills incorporating many of these areas have been considered: H.R. 2848, the Department of State Operations and Embassy Security Authorization Act, Fiscal Year 2014, and S. 1386, the Chris Stevens, Sean Smith, Tyrone Woods, and Glen Doherty Embassy Security, Threat Mitigation, and Personnel Protection Act of 2013.

The 113th Congress, through the Consolidated Appropriations Act of 2014, has also fully funded the Administration's FY2014 request for diplomatic security-related accounts, providing approximately $5.4 billion.

This report briefly summarizes and tracks congressional and State Department actions in response to the attack, and will be updated as necessary to reflect further developments and actions on ongoing policy proposals. Readers seeking background information on recent embassy attacks, State Department policies and procedures relevant to embassy security, or information on recent year embassy security funding trends should consult CRS Report R42834, *Securing U.S. Diplomatic Facilities and Personnel Abroad: Background and Policy Issues*.

Contents

Figures

Tables

Appendixes

Contacts

Introduction

While attacks on U.S. diplomatic facilities and personnel abroad are not infrequent,[1] the severity of the September 11, 2012, attack on U.S. facilities in Benghazi, Libya, has caused a reexamination of measures in place to protect U.S. diplomatic personnel and facilities abroad. Ambassador Christopher Stevens was the first sitting U.S. ambassador to have been killed since 1979. Moreover, a concern exists that the attack may reflect a growing danger to U.S. diplomatic facilities—the result of an increasingly diffuse threat from extremists across the Middle East and of Arab revolutions that have decreased the capacity, and perhaps the will, of local governments to protect U.S. interests. Congressional and State Department actions will be critical to responding to this evolving threat and to preventing similar tragedies in the future.

Congress has legislated extensive changes to the U.S. approach to securing facilities and personnel in at least two previous instances of attacks on U.S. diplomatic facilities abroad. The 1983-1984 bombings of U.S. facilities in Beirut, Lebanon, led to the adoption of the Omnibus Diplomatic Security and Antiterrorism Act of 1986,[2] which, among other measures, established the State Department's Bureau of Diplomatic Security. Similarly, the 1998 bombings of U.S. embassies in Kenya and Tanzania led to, among other measures, a significant construction funding program under the Secure Embassy Construction and Counterterrorism Act of 1999 (SECCA).[3]

After the Benghazi attack, Congress initiated oversight through investigations by several committees and through a number of hearings featuring testimony from officials ranging from the working level to the Secretary of State. Members have also put forward a number of legislative proposals on issues ranging from the composition of Accountability Review Boards to procedures for awarding contracts for local security guards. Two of these measures have been considered and approved by committees.

The Department of State undertook several measures in response to the attack, including immediate steps to bolster security at posts around the world; an investigation of the incident through an Accountability Review Board; and longer-term measures implementing the board's recommendations, including requests for significantly greater funding than in recent years.

The following summarizes and tracks congressional and State Department efforts to make U.S. embassies and personnel around the world more secure. It will be updated as necessary to reflect further developments and actions on ongoing policy proposals.[4]

---

[1] There were 521 attacks on U.S. diplomatic embassies, consulates, or personnel in 92 countries between 1970 and 2012, according to the National Consortium for the Study of Terrorism and Responses to Terrorism (START). The incidents led to nearly 500 deaths. See Erin Miller, *August 2013 Security Threat to Americans Abroad*, The National Consortium for the Study of Terrorism and Responses to Terrorism (START), Background Report, August 2013, p. 3, http://www.start.umd.edu/start/publications/br/STARTBackgroundReport_Aug2013SecurityThreats.pdf.

[2] 22 U.S.C. §4801 et seq., P.L. 99-399.

[3] H.R. 3427, which was enacted as Title VI of Appendix G of P.L. 106-113.

[4] The responses of U.S. government agencies other than the Department of State to the Benghazi attack are not covered in this report, unless noted.

Department of State Actions in Response to the Benghazi Attack

The protection of U.S. government employees and facilities under chief of mission authority overseas from terrorist, criminal, or technical attack is the responsibility of the Secretary of State.[5] The Benghazi attack prompted the State Department to take several actions. In the immediate aftermath, the department ordered all posts to review their security posture and to take all necessary steps to enhance it if necessary.[6] Shortly thereafter, five Interagency Security Assessment Teams (ISATs) were deployed to 19 posts in 13 countries to undertake urgent reviews of high-threat posts.[7]

In order to ensure consistent focus on the most endangered locations, State also reorganized its Diplomatic Security Bureau by establishing a new Deputy Assistant Secretary for High Threat Posts to oversee security arrangements for a number of so-designated countries. While press reports initially suggested the department had designated 17 High Threat Posts, State officials have suggested that this number is not static and that it would be reconsidered annually, at a minimum. As of mid-July 2013, the number of High Threat Posts stood at 28.[8]

The Benghazi Accountability Review Board

In addition to the above steps, in the first week of October 2012, then-Secretary of State Clinton convened an accountability review board (ARB) to investigate the Benghazi attack.[9] The board was chaired by former Under Secretary of State Thomas Pickering and included five members, four of whom were designated by the Secretary of State and one by the intelligence community.[10]

On December 18, the Benghazi Accountability Review Board published its findings in an unclassified version of its report.[11] The board concluded that, while responsibility for the attack rests solely and completely with the terrorists who perpetrated it, systemic failures in Washington led to key decisions that left the Special Mission in Benghazi with significant security shortfalls. Key leadership failures in the Bureau of Diplomatic Security (DS) as well as in the Bureau of Near Eastern Affairs (NEA) led to confusion over decision-making in relation to security and

---

[5] 22 U.S.C. §4802, P.L. 99-399.

[6] Transcript, State Department Briefing to Update on Recent Events in Libya, September 12, 2012.

[7] See U.S. Congress, House Committee on Foreign Affairs, *Benghazi Attack, Part II: The Report of the Accountability Review Board*, 112th Cong., 2nd sess., December 20, 2012; and U.S. Congress, Senate Committee on Foreign Relations, *Benghazi: The Attack and the Lessons Learned*, 112th Cong., December 20, 2012.

[8] See Bill Miller, Deputy Assistant Secretary of State for High Threat Posts, Testimony before the Senate Foreign Relations Committee, July 16, 2013.

[9] As required by Title III of the Omnibus Diplomatic and Antiterrorism Act of 1986, 22 U.S.C. §4831 et seq.

[10] The other members of the board were: Admiral Michael Mullen (Ret), a former Chairman of the Joint Chiefs of Staff; Richard Shinnick, a retired Senior Foreign Service Officer who served as interim Director for the Department of State's Bureau of Overseas Buildings Operations in 2008; Catherine Bertini, a Professor of Public Administration and International Affairs at the Maxwell School of Citizenship and Public Affairs and former Executive Director of the United Nations World Food Program; and Hugh Turner, a former deputy director of the CIA's Directorate of Operations.

[11] Department of State, *Accountability Review Board for Benghazi Attack of September 2012*, December 19, 2012, http://www.state.gov/documents/organization/202446.pdf.

policy in Benghazi; these were likely factors in the insufficient priority given to the Benghazi mission's security-related requests, according to the board. Still, these leadership failures did not amount to a clear breach of duty by any single U.S. government employee, the board found.

The board also determined that decisions by the Department's senior leadership regarding the nature and extension of Special Mission Benghazi's unclear status left it outside normal procedures for funding and executing security measures, including office facility standards and accountability measures under the Secure Embassy Construction and Counterterrorism Act of 1999[12] and the Overseas Security Policy Board (OSPB).[13]

State Department Implementation of ARB Recommendations

On the release of the ARB's report, the Department of State accepted the panel's recommendations and pledged to implement them fully. The department formed a task force to implement the board's 29 recommendations, as they were translated into 64 specific action items assigned to bureaus for implementation.

In reviewing failures of leadership and management, the department removed four of its employees from the positions they held at the time of the attack. The officials removed from their positions include three officials from the Bureau of Diplomatic Security and one from the Bureau of Near Eastern Affairs. The four State Department employees, who had been on administrative leave, were returned to duty on August 20 and reassigned to other positions within the department.[14] Prior to the officials' reinstatement, a number of Members of Congress had sought clarification on their administrative status, in order to assess whether the department had held the appropriate officials to account in a full and fair manner.[15] In addition, while the ARB fixed responsibility for these failures at the level of Assistant Secretary and below, some congressional observers have suggested that more senior department officials should have been held more fully to account.

By January 2013, then-Secretary Clinton reported to Congress that, of the ARB's recommendations, "more than 80 percent are on track to be completed by the end of March, with a number completed already."[16] Later, Secretary of State Kerry also stated that as Secretary, he is "committed to implementing every single one of the recommendations in the report of the Accountability Review Board and doing more."[17]

The department described its progress in implementing the ARB's recommendations in a fact sheet first released on May 20, 2013, and updated on September 11, 2013, and January 15, 2014;

---

[12] H.R. 3427, which was enacted as Title VI of Appendix G of P.L. 106-113.

[13] More information on the board's extensive findings and recommendations is available in CRS Report R42834, *Securing U.S. Diplomatic Facilities and Personnel Abroad: Background and Policy Issues*.

[14] Department of State, Daily Press Briefing, August 20, 2013.

[15] See Letter from Edward R. Royce, Chairman of the House Foreign Affairs Committee, and 14 other Members of the Committee to The Honorable John F. Kerry, Secretary of State, May 29, 2013.

[16] Department of State, *Report to the Congress on Actions Taken by the Department of State In Response to the Program Recommendations of the Accountability Review Board on the Death of Four Official Americans in Benghazi, Libya September 11, 2012*, January 2013.

[17] Secretary of State John Kerry, *Remarks to the Foreign Service Institute Overseas Security Seminar*, Department of State, May 20, 2013, http://www.state.gov/secretary/remarks/2013/05/209671 htm.

the text of the updated fact sheet is included as **Appendix A**. The document stated that the department had addressed or was addressing all 24 unclassified recommendations. It also indicated that 113 new diplomatic security personnel (including 75 DS agents) had been hired by the Department of State by the end of September, with the remaining 38 expected to be hired in FY2014. The department reportedly also expected 90 additional Marine guards to deploy to high-risk embassies by the end of 2013.[18]

In accordance with the Benghazi ARB's recommendations, the department convened a panel of external security experts in April 2013 to identify best practices from other agencies and countries. The so-called *Best Practices Panel*, chaired by former Director of U.S. Secret Service Mark Sullivan, reportedly provided its report to the department in late August 2013. The panel observed that many security-related decisions were in the hands of the Department of State's Under Secretary for Management, a position overseeing what it viewed as a too-large number of support functions, creating what it deemed a "span of control" problem. Accordingly, the panel's chief recommendation was the elevation of the diplomatic security function through the creation of an Under Secretary for Diplomatic Security, which would focus all security issues through a single focal point at the senior executive level, according to press reports.[19]

An additional panel of outside experts was charged by the department with a thorough "review [of] DS's organization and management structure." This panel, chaired by former Under Secretary of State for Management Grant Green, reportedly delivered its findings to the Under Secretary of State for Management in May 2013.[20] The report has not been made public, but the department's updated January 15, 2014, fact sheet in **Appendix A** states that 4 of the 35 recommendations made by the report's authors were not accepted by State. According to Acting Assistant Secretary for Diplomatic Security Gregory Starr, the department disagrees with recommendations pertaining to the need for a Chief of Staff for Diplomatic Security, and regarding the nature of the DS threat analysis office (whether it should be considered part of the intelligence community or a consumer of intelligence products).[21]

Funding Requests

In response to the ARB report as well as its own internal post-Benghazi assessments, the Department of State requested additional funding from Congress to improve its security measures for both FY2013 and FY2014. As part of what it termed an Increased Security Proposal (ISP), State in December 2012 submitted a revised FY2013 budget request to Congress outlining resource shifts totaling approximately $1.419 billion, primarily a reallocation of unobligated funds originally intended for programs in Iraq. The request sought $553 million for 35 new detachments of Marine Security Guards (roughly 225 Marines) to medium- and high-threat posts

---

[18] Eric Schmitt, "U.S. Takes Steps to Add Security at Embassies," *The New York Times*, May 20, 2013.

[19] Department of State, *Report of the Independent Panel on Best Practices*, as released by Al Jazeera America, September 4, 2013, p. 13, http://america.aljazeera.com/articles/2013/9/3/exclusive-benghazireportdetailssecurityflawsatusdiplomaticposts html. See also Eric Schmitt, "Diplomatic Security Must Be Priority at State Dept., Panel Says," *The New York Times*, September 4, 2013.

[20] United States Department of State and the Broadcasting Board of Governors Office of Inspector General, *Special Review of the Accountability Review Board Process*, ISP-I-13-44A, September 25, 2013, p. 24, http://oig.state.gov/documents/organization/214907.pdf.

[21] Gregory Starr, Acting Assistant Secretary of State for Diplomatic Security, testimony before the Senate Foreign Relations Committee, September 19, 2013.

to serve as visible deterrents to hostile acts;[22] $130 million to increase the size of the Diplomatic Security workforce by 155 DS personnel, mostly focused on medium- and high-threat posts; and $736 million to fund facility security upgrades and construction of new embassy compounds.[23]

The Administration's FY2014 budget request seeks to sustain the initiatives launched under the FY2013 Increased Security Proposal, including expansion of the Bureau of Diplomatic Security and further growth in the number of Marine Security Guard detachments deployed to diplomatic facilities. The request seeks $2.2 billion for construction of new secure diplomatic facilities, a combination of enduring funding, Overseas Contingency Operations (OCO) funding, and other agency contributions. The request for Embassy Security, Construction and Maintenance of $2.65 billion (including $250 million in OCO) represents a 60% increase from the FY2012 actual level. Within this account, Worldwide Security Upgrades funding (for bricks and mortar security needs, including construction of secure new embassy compounds) would grow by 108% to $1.61 billion, while Ongoing Operations would increase by 18%. Worldwide Security Protection funds (for security programs including a worldwide guard force), under Diplomatic and Consular Programs, would rise by 37%, to $2.18 billion. President Obama issued a statement on May 16, 2013, calling on Congress to "fully fund Embassy security" and support implementation of the ARB recommendations.[24]

Among its funding-related prescriptions, the ARB recommended that "the State Department must work with Congress to restore the Capital Security Cost Sharing (CSCS) Program at its full capacity, adjusted for inflation to approximately $2.2 billion in fiscal year 2015, including an up to ten-year program addressing that need, prioritized for construction of new facilities in high risk, high threat areas."[25] The Capital Security Cost Sharing Program requires all U.S. agencies with presence at diplomatic facilities abroad (including the State Department) to pay a share toward the cost of those facilities. The size of each agency's required contribution is directly linked with the number of positions it authorizes overseas.[26] In its FY2014 budget request, the department accordingly seeks $1.4 billion for the restoration of the CSCS. **Figure 1** depicts this request in the context of recent year funding levels. Additional information about recent year funding requests and levels is available in CRS Report R42834, *Securing U.S. Diplomatic Facilities and Personnel Abroad: Background and Policy Issues.*

---

[22] Gregory Starr, Acting Assistant Secretary of State for Diplomatic Security, testified before the Senate Foreign Relations Committee on September 19, 2013, that the deployment of all 35 new Marine Security Guard detachments would likely be a three-year process.

[23] Congress provided the Department of State with the authority to transfer more than $1 billion from Iraq Operations OCO funds to accounts addressing global security needs within the context of the FY2013 Consolidated and Further Continuing Appropriations Act, 2013 (P.L. 113-6, §1708).

[24] The White House, "President Obama Calls on Congress to Fully Fund Embassy Security," press release, May 16, 2013, http://www.whitehouse.gov/the-press-office/2013/05/16/president-obama-calls-congress-fully-fund-embassy-security.

[25] Department of State, *Report of the Accountability Review Board on the Benghazi Attack*, December 19, 2012, p. 9.

[26] The Capital Security Cost Sharing program was authorized by the Secure Embassy Construction and Counterterrorism Act of 1999 (SECCA), H.R. 3427, enacted as Title VI of Appendix G of P.L. 106-113, and amended by §629 of P.L. 108-447.

Figure 1. Capital Security Cost Sharing Program Funding, FY2010-FY2014

($ in current millions; Department of State contributions only)

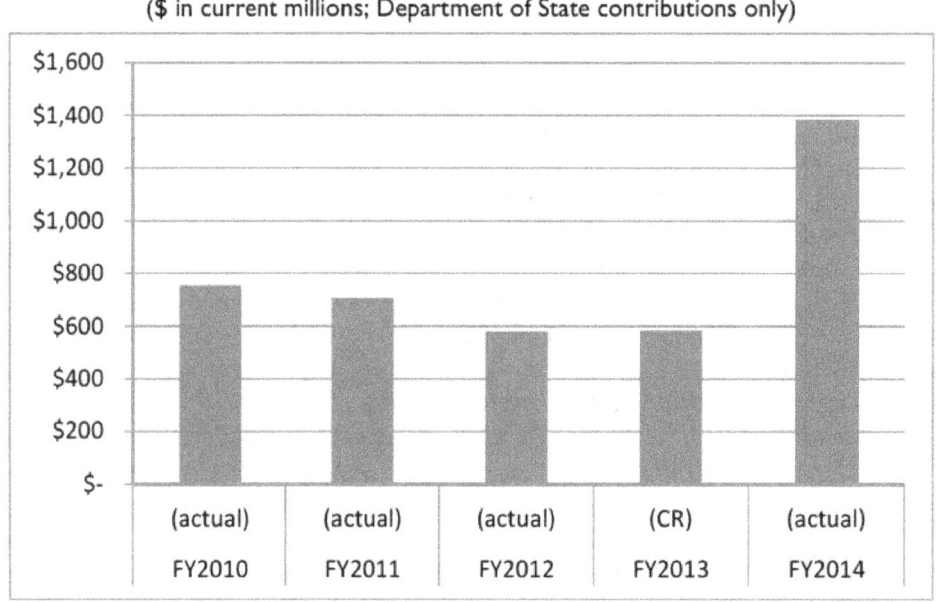

Source: Department of State Congressional Budget Justifications, FY2012-FY2014; H.R. 3547 Explanatory Statement, *Congressional Record*, January 15, 2014, pp. H1162.

Legislative Response to the Benghazi Attack

Congressional activity in the 112th and 113th Congresses on the issue of the protection of U.S. personnel and facilities abroad has included a number of legislative actions and proposals, as well as a variety of hearings and investigations into the Benghazi attack by a number of different committees.[27]

Legislative Investigations and Oversight

Congress has produced three publicly released reports pertaining to the Benghazi attack. The first was presented in the 112th Congress by the Senate Committee on Homeland Security and Governmental Affairs' Chairman Joseph Lieberman and Ranking Member Susan Collins on December 30, 2012.[28] Their report found that the Department of State did not take sufficiently into account clear evidence of a worsening security situation in Benghazi and requests for additional support from U.S. personnel posted there. This situation was compounded by the evident inability of the Libyan government to perform its duty to protect U.S. diplomatic facilities

---

[27] Additional actions and statements by Members of Congress not specifically pertaining to hearings or legislation are not covered in detail in this report. Most recently, for example, Senator Lindsey Graham announced on October 28, 2013, that he would "block every appointment in the U.S. Senate" until the survivors of the Benghazi attack were made available to Congress. On October 30, 2013, House Homeland Security Chairman Michael McCaul and 84 cosigners sent a letter to Secretary of State John Kerry questioning why the State Department's Rewards for Justice Program had not been activated to facilitate the apprehension of the perpetrators of the Benghazi attack.

[28] U.S. Congress, Senate Committee on Homeland Security and Governmental Affairs, *Flashing Red: A Special Report on the Terrorist Attacks at Benghazi*, By Joseph I. Lieberman, chairman, and Susan M. Collins, ranking Member, 112th Cong., 2nd sess., December 30, 2012.

and personnel. In this context, the department should have increased protective measures or withdrawn the U.S. presence there, even without specific intelligence about an imminent attack, the report concludes. The Senate report's recommendations included additional interagency joint assessments of the security requirements of high-risk U.S. diplomatic facilities; a funding process delivering sufficient, steady, and timely funding to secure diplomatic facilities and personnel worldwide; additional Department of Defense (DOD) assets and personnel devoted to the African continent; and clear and consistent communication by Administration officials about terrorist attacks.

A second report was put forward on April 23, 2013, when the chairmen of five House committees active in the 113th Congress in oversight of the Benghazi attack presented to the House Republican Conference an "Interim Progress Report" on their inquiries.[29] Among the report's preliminary findings were that the senior leadership of the Department of State approved security reductions at the Benghazi diplomatic facilities prior to the 9/11/12 attack, and that the public presentation of the attack by the Administration was deliberately inaccurate in order to protect State Department interests. The report relates the chairmen's view that continued examination and oversight by their respective committees of the Benghazi attack, and the Administration's response to it, remain necessary.

On January 15, 2014, the Senate Select Committee on Intelligence issued its *Review on the Terrorist Attacks on U.S. Facilities in Benghazi, Libya, September 11-12, 2012*.[30] The report concludes that the attacks were likely preventable, based on known security shortfalls at the State Department facility in Benghazi, and based on extensive intelligence reporting on terrorist activity in Libya. The report includes 14 findings, ranging from the alarming pre-attack strategic intelligence picture, to the absence of U.S. military assets positioned to intervene rapidly; and 18 recommendations on issues including security standards, intelligence capabilities and processes, the use of local security guards, and the need to bring the attackers to justice, among others.

A number of committees have held hearings relating to the Benghazi attack; a list of selected hearings focused on the Benghazi attack is available in **Appendix B**.[31] However, some Members have suggested that effective oversight would require the creation of a select committee to investigate and report on the Benghazi attack. H.Res. 36, introduced by Representative Frank Wolf on January 18, 2013, would establish such a committee and set out its purpose, composition, and procedures. The measure had 180 cosponsors as of February 3, 2014. S.Res. 225, introduced by Senator Ted Cruz on September 12, 2013, would express the sense of the Senate that Congress should establish a joint select committee to investigate and report on the attack; the measure had 24 cosponsors as of February 3, 2014. Those who support the proposal tout the additional, across-

---

[29] The report, by Chairman Howard P. "Buck" McKeon, Committee on Armed Services; Chairman Ed Royce, Committee on Foreign Affairs; Chairman Bob Goodlatte, Committee on the Judiciary; Chairman Darrell Issa, Committee on Oversight & Government Reform; Chairman Mike Rogers, Permanent Select Committee on Intelligence, is available on-line at http://oversight.house.gov/wp-content/uploads/2013/04/Libya-Progress-Report-Final-1.pdf.

[30] U.S. Congress, Senate Select Committee on Intelligence, *Review of the Terrorist Attacks on U.S. Facilities in Benghazi, Libya, September 11-12, 2012*, together with Additional Views, 113th Cong., January 15, 2014, http://www.intelligence.senate.gov/benghazi2014/benghazi.pdf.

[31] Not all Committee activities are included in this summary. For example, according to one report, two Diplomatic Security agents (Alec Henderson and John Martinec) who witnessed the Benghazi attack appeared before House Committee on Oversight and Government Reform staff on October 8, 2013. See Richard A. Serrano, "Benghazi witnesses grilled in secret on Capitol Hill," *Los Angeles Times*, October 28, 2013.

government subpoena powers afforded the chairman of a select committee, and suggest that the current approach suffers from being fractured across committee jurisdictions.[32] The House Speaker has publicly opposed the measure.[33]

Diplomatic Security Legislation in the 113th Congress

In the 113th Congress to date, two bills relating directly to embassy security matters have been considered and approved by committees in the House and Senate (in addition to bills to appropriate FY2014 funds for the Department of State, including diplomatic security accounts, that have also received House and Senate committee action):

1. H.R. 2848, the Department of State Operations and Embassy Security Authorization Act, Fiscal Year 2014, introduced by House Foreign Affairs Committee Chairman Royce on July 30, 2013, considered and approved by voice vote by the House Foreign Affairs Committee on August 1, and passed by the House on September 29.[34]

2. S. 1386, the Chris Stevens, Sean Smith, Tyrone Woods, and Glen Doherty Embassy Security, Threat Mitigation, and Personnel Protection Act of 2013, introduced by Senate Foreign Relations Committee Chairman Menendez on July 30, 2013; adopted by voice vote and ordered reported favorably to the full Senate on August 1.

Prior to the committees' consideration of these measures, a number of other legislative proposals related to the Benghazi attack and its implications for the protection of U.S. personnel and facilities abroad had been introduced and are listed in **Appendix C**. The two bills that have been considered by committees, H.R. 2848 and S. 1386, both would impact related policy matters. However, their provisions differ significantly, and the following sections compare their main elements.

Table 1. H.R. 2848 and S. 1386 Legislative Status (as of February 2014)

Full Committee Markup		H.R. 2848 Report	House Passage	S. 1386 Report	Senate Passage	Conf. Report	Conference Report Approval		Public Law
H.R. 2848	S. 1386						House	Senate	
08/01/2013	08/01/2013	H.Rept. 113-226	09/29/2013						

Source: CRS.

---

[32] Guy Taylor, "Republicans weigh risks, benefits of select committee on Benghazi," *The Washington Times*, May 19, 2013.

[33] When asked about the possibility of a special committee on Benghazi, House Speaker Boehner told Fox News on May 22, 2013 that "I don't think at this point in time that it's necessary. Now, we may get to a point where it is. But at this point, I think our committees are doing a very good job, and I'm going to be supportive of them."

[34] H.R. 2848 also includes a number of foreign affairs authorization measures not relating directly to embassy security issues; those measures are not covered in this report.

Funding

H.R. 2848 authorizes $2.65 billion for FY2014 for the Department of State's Embassy Security, Construction, and Maintenance (ESCM) account, and $2.18 billion for Worldwide Security Protection. It also permits the transfer of additional funds to the ESCM account after consultation with appropriate committees.

S. 1386 authorizes for FY2014:

- $1.383 billion for the Capital Security Cost Sharing Program, of which $300 million would go to immediate threat mitigation at high-threat, high-risk posts;

- $5 million for language training for diplomatic security personnel at high-threat, high-risk posts;

- $100 million for improved training facilities for high-threat, high-risk post personnel, as well as $350 million for the acquisition, construction, and operation of a new Foreign Affairs Security Training Center, and $54.54 million of American Reinvestment and Recovery Act of 2009 (P.L. 111-5) funds also to be applied to improved training facilities.

H.R. 3547, the Consolidated Appropriations Act of 2014, exceeds the Administration's request for Embassy Security, Construction, and Maintenance of $2.4 billion by $25 million in OCO funds, to be used to harden high-risk posts. It also provides a total of $2.77 billion for Worldwide Security Protection (of which $0.90 billion are OCO funds), specifying that the $585 million above the requested amount should be applied to the normalization of Iraq operations. When compared to FY2013 levels, however, the ESCM account shows a reduction of 5.5% (or approximately $155 million). Worldwide Security Protection funds for FY2014 would grow by $517 million, or 23%, over FY2013 levels.

Accountability Review Board Process

While the Administration has asserted that the Benghazi Accountability Review Board was independent and thorough, some congressional observers have suggested that the ARB process is fundamentally flawed. Some observers have questioned whether an investigative body made up principally of current and former officials of the institution under investigation can truly be independent. Others argue that oversight of the ARB process is made more difficult by the absence of a requirement that ARB reports be provided directly to Congress. Finally, public scrutiny of the process is made more difficult by the classification of nearly all previous ARB reports, some suggest.

A number of measures have been introduced in the House seeking to reform the process by which accountability review boards are conducted. H.R. 1768, the Accountability Review Board Reform Act of 2013, would amend the 1986 Diplomatic Security Act to increase the independence of ARBs from the State Department through, among other measures, changing the composition of the membership of ARBs (under current statute, four members named by the Secretary of State and one named by the Director of National Intelligence) to have fewer State-appointed members, and specifying conflict of interest guidelines. Although H.R. 2848 does not include these measures, Chairman Royce has reportedly stated his intent to take up more comprehensive review of the ARB process in the fall of 2013.[35]

S. 1386 describes the current ARB mechanism as an effective tool. Still, it proposes reforms to the membership of ARB panels, requiring that the Department of State's Inspector General serve as one of State's four appointees to ARBs. It would also require that the staff supporting any given ARB should not be drawn from bureaus or units impacted by the incident under review. Finally, it calls for ARB reports to be provided directly to Congress, not later than two days after it is provided to the Secretary of State (under current statute, the report itself is not required to be shared with Congress).

Personnel Accountability

The Benghazi Accountability Review Board found that significant leadership failures contributed to the gravity of the event; however, the board assessed that such failures did not amount to a clear breach of duty by any single U.S. government employee. It therefore did not recommend disciplinary action against any individual. The Benghazi ARB recommended clarifying the authority of future boards to empower them to recommend disciplinary action in cases of unsatisfactory leadership by senior officials.

Both H.R. 2848 and S. 1386 take up this recommendation to broaden the standard by which future boards can recommend discipline. H.R. 2848 takes up a measure originally introduced as H.R. 925, the Securing Accountability in Foreign Embassies (SAFE Embassies) Act, which would require an ARB to recommend investigatory or disciplinary action if it found that an individual's misconduct or unsatisfactory performance of duty significantly contributed to serious injury, loss of life, significant property destruction, or serious security breach at or related to a U.S. government mission abroad.

The related measure in S. 1386, originally proposed as Section 203 of S. 980, appears somewhat narrower in scope than the House measure. It would allow ARBs to recommend disciplinary action on the basis of unsatisfactory leadership by a senior official with respect to a security incident involving loss of life, serious injury, or significant destruction of property at or related to a U.S. government mission abroad.

Contracting

The Department of State has requested authority to allow it to use best-value contracting for local guard contracts, rather than "lowest price technically acceptable" criteria.[36] Current statute requires the department to award contracts using a lowest price technically acceptable selection

---

[35] Carolyn Phenicie, "Embassy Security Provisions Advance With Panel's State Department Bill," *Congressional Quarterly Roll Call*, August 1, 2013.

[36] For background on how best value and best price approaches to local security guard contracts impact the Department of State, see United States Department of State and the Broadcasting Board of Governors Office of Inspector General, *Review of Best-Value Contracting for the Department of State Local Guard Program and the Utility of Expanding the Policy Beyond High-Threat Posts in Iraq, Afghanistan, and Pakistan*, AUD/CG-12-27, February 29, 2012, http://oig.state.gov/documents/organization/185288.pdf.

---

process, with exceptions for Iraq, Afghanistan, and Pakistan.[37] A "best value" approach would allow other factors, such as prior performance, to be included in the review of a bid.

Legislative measures have been introduced in both the House and Senate on this subject. H.R. 2848 took up a measure outlined in H.R. 731, the Protecting Americans Abroad Act, which would authorize the State Department to use a best value contracting award method for local guard forces when deemed necessary in high-risk areas. S. 1386 took up a similar provision (from S. 980) which would allow the Secretary of State to award contracts on the basis of best value; however, it would not be geographically limited. Both bills would also require the department to report each instance of "best value" contracting to relevant committees.

This measure was taken up as Section 7006 of H.R. 3547, the Consolidated Appropriations Act of 2014, which authorizes the Secretary of State to award local guard contracts for high-risk, high-threat posts on the basis of best value as determined by a cost-technical tradeoff analysis.

High-Threat Posts: Assessment and Reporting

H.R. 2848 would require the Secretary of State to submit a list of high-risk, high-threat posts within 30 days of the enactment of this section, in classified form. It also would require the Secretary to regularly review existing and potential posts to determine whether they should be included in this category. Under the measure, when opening or reopening such a post, the Secretary must convene a working group that would evaluate the rationale for the post; ensure proper funding, physical security measures, and personnel are provided to the post; and establish "tripwires" that might trigger a change to the post's status (such as an evacuation of non-essential personnel, or a closure). The Secretary would also be required to notify Congress not less than 30 days before opening or reopening such a post.

S. 1386, on the other hand, would require the Secretary to submit a report within 90 days evaluating high-threat, high-risk facilities, including detailed information on the threats to and staffing at the post, as well as host nation capabilities and willingness to defend it. It also requires a summary of all security requests regarding each high threat, high risk post during the previous calendar year. The State Department Inspector General's Office would also be charged with reviewing the designation of such posts, as well as contingency planning, risk mitigation and early warning systems pertaining to such posts, and reporting its assessments to Congress.

Security Training

H.R. 2848 requires personnel assigned to high-risk, high-threat posts to receive security training to help them cope with potential attacks. In addition, it requires senior officials who might be in a management role at high-risk, high-threat posts to receive training on threat evaluation and the effective identification and application of resources to address those threats. Finally, it calls for diplomatic security personnel assigned to high risk, high threat posts to receive adequate language training to allow them to better manage discussions with locals regarding security matters.

S. 1386 addresses similar ground regarding Department of State personnel training; however, it does so by authorizing $100 million for improved training facilities for high-risk, high-threat post

---

[37] 22 U.S.C. §4864.

personnel, as well as $350 million for the acquisition, construction, and operation of a Foreign Affairs Security Training Center. $54.54 million of American Reinvestment and Recovery Act of 2009 (P.L. 111-5) funds are also to be applied to improved training facilities. The measure would also authorize $5 million for language training for diplomatic security personnel at high-risk, high-threat posts.

Marine Security Guard Program

The Marine Security Guard Program is a collaborative effort between the Departments of Defense and State. In the wake of the Benghazi attack, the Secretary of Defense was directed to grow the Marine Security Guard program in order to increase the number of detachments at United States embassies, consulates, and other diplomatic facilities by up to 1,000 Marines during Fiscal Years 2014 through 2017, and reassess the program's focus on the protection of classified information.[38] The President must also separate the program's budget request from that of the Marine Corps as a whole; and it requires reexamination of the Marine units' rules of engagement.

The Department of State also intends to expand its participation in the Marine Security Guard program. Accordingly, S. 1386 requires the Secretary of State (in consultation with the Secretary of Defense) to elaborate and implement a plan to incorporate the additional Marine Security Guard teams required by the FY2013 NDAA. Under the measure, the Secretary would also bear responsibility (in consultation with the Secretary of Defense) for an annual review of the program's size and composition, as well as an assessment of the adequacy of the distribution of marine teams to posts, and an evaluation of the objectives of the program and its rules of engagement. H.R. 2848 calls for a similar annual review of the program.

Additional Measures

The House and Senate measures each have additional provisions. H.R. 2848 requires the Departments of State and Defense to jointly develop contingency plans for attacks at high-risk, high-threat posts; requires the Secretary of State to conduct a Strategic Review of the Bureau of Diplomatic Security; authorizes the Secretary to make physical security enhancements at schools where children of government-employed U.S. citizens attend; and directs the Secretary to station key personnel at high-risk, high-threat posts for sustained periods of time.

S. 1386 would also specify a number of qualifications for the Deputy Assistant Secretary of State for High Threat, High Risk Posts; require regular briefings on State's Security Environment Threat List; require reporting on risks at posts in high counterintelligence threat nations; and require a report by the Comptroller General on the progress made by the Department of State in implementing the Benghazi ARB's recommendations.

---

[38] H.R. 4310 (P.L. 112-239), "National Defense Authorization Act for Fiscal Year 2013," Title IV, Subtitle A, Section 404, "Additional Marine Corps Personnel for the Marine Corps Security Guard Program."

Appendix A. Department of State Fact Sheet on Benghazi ARB Implementation

<u>Title</u>: Fact Sheet: Benghazi Accountability Review Board Implementation

<u>Source</u>: U.S. Department of State Office of the Spokesperson, January 15, 2014

http://www.state.gov/r/pa/prs/ps/2014/01/
219760.htm_____

_____

Following the September 11, 2012 attack on U.S. government facilities in Benghazi, Libya, the independent Benghazi Accountability Review Board (ARB) on December 19, 2012, issued 29 recommendations (24 of which were unclassified) to the Department of State. The department accepted each of the ARB's recommendations and is committed to implementing them. This will require fundamentally reforming the organization in critical ways – work which is already well underway. While risk can never be completely eliminated from our diplomatic and development duties, we must always work to minimize it. A brief update of the department's actions on the 24 unclassified recommendations is as follows:

Unclassified Recommendations of the ARB (Text abridged) and *Department Actions*

OVERARCHING SECURITY CONSIDERATIONS

1. The Department must strengthen security for personnel and platforms beyond traditional reliance on host government security support in high risk, high threat posts.

- Hard decisions must be made when it comes to whether the United States should operate in dangerous overseas locations. We are refining an institutionalized, repeatable, and transparent process to make risk-managed decisions regarding the U.S. presence at high-threat locations, including whether to begin, restart, continue, modify the current staffing footprint, or cease operations.

- We are creating a "Security Accountability Framework" that clearly defines key actors, their roles and responsibilities, and governance mechanisms. This framework will provide an essential foundation for implementing our new risk management methodologies.

- We created a Deputy Assistant Secretary for High Threat Programs in the Bureau of Diplomatic Security (DS), who is responsible for ensuring that high-threat posts receive the focused attention they need.

2. The Board recommends that the Department re-examine DS organization and management, with a particular emphasis on span of control for security policy planning for all overseas U.S. diplomatic facilities.

- The Department established a six-person panel to thoroughly review DS's organization and management structure.

- The panel concluded its work on May 3, 2013, making 35 recommendations to improve DS operations and its management structure. The Department accepted

31 of these recommendations and is working to implementing them. Recommendations include:

- Reviewing Diplomatic Security allocation both domestically and abroad to ensure priority positions overseas are filled first;

- Establishing a Diplomatic Security strategic planning unit; and,

- Continuing to pursue a Diplomatic Security training complement to combat the problem faced by managers who are not able to replace personnel attending their required training.

3. Regional bureaus should have augmented support within the bureau on security matters, to include a senior DS officer to report to the regional Assistant Secretary.

- DS staff attend regular Regional Bureau meetings, and Regional Bureau staff attend DS daily briefings to better communicate on security issues.

- The Department has adjusted the work requirements (position descriptions) for senior level staff (Assistant Secretaries and Deputy Assistant Secretaries) to reflect everyone's shared responsibility for overseas security.

4. The Department should establish a panel of outside independent experts (military, security, humanitarian) with experience in high risk, high threat areas to identify best practices (from other agencies and other countries), and evaluate U.S. security platforms in high risk, high threat posts.

- The Department established a five-person panel to identify best practices used by other agencies and countries.

- The Best Practices Panel transmitted its final report to the Department in September 2013.

- The panel made 40 recommendations, which are under consideration by the Department. We expect to implement 39 of 40 recommendations.

- Many recommendations built upon those made by the Benghazi ARB including: establishing a Department-wide risk management model and policy; increased hard-skills training for the foreign affairs community; and developing a security accountability framework.

5. The Department should develop minimum security standards for occupancy of temporary facilities in high risk, high threat environments, and seek greater flexibility to make funds rapidly available for security upgrades at such facilities.

- The Department has re-affirmed that Overseas Security Policy Board Standards apply to all facilities.

- Working with Congress, the Department identified flexible funding authorities in the Increased Security Proposal to make improvements to our overseas facilities.

6. Before opening or re-opening critical threat or high risk, high threat posts, the Department should establish a multi-bureau support cell, residing in the regional bureau.

- The Department developed standard operating procedures for "Support Cells" for opened/reopened posts.

- The process has been incorporated into the Foreign Affairs Handbook at 2 FAM 420; the FAM covers both regular and high-threat posts, and clearly sets out the actions to be taken by relevant bureaus and offices.

7. All State Department and other government agencies' facilities should be collocated when they are in the same metropolitan area, unless a waiver has been approved.

- We verified all data on our overseas facilities; we are exploring which non-collocated facilities can be eliminated and their personnel relocated.

- When new facilities are planned and built, they are done so with all approved staff being collocated, unless a waiver is in place.

8. The Secretary should require an action plan from Diplomatic Security, Overseas Buildings Operations, and other relevant offices on the use of fire as a weapon against diplomatic facilities, including immediate steps to deal with urgent issues.

- The Department issued guidance to all posts on "weapons of opportunity."

- Fire testing is ongoing at U.S. military facilities.

- We have developed training that addresses survival in smoke and fire situations.

9. The Department should revise its guidance to posts and require key offices to perform in-depth status checks of post tripwires.

- The Department reviewed and revised requirements for posts on how to respond to changing security benchmarks (i.e., "tripwires").

- The Department established a Washington-based "Tripwires Committee" to review tripwires upon breach, to help ensure that posts and regional bureaus in Washington respond more quickly should security deteriorate at post.

- To allow Washington to track and respond to breached tripwires overseas, the Department developed an application called ALERT (Action Log for Emergency Response to Tripwires).

- The Department also uses ALERT to review all tripwires of high-threat, high risk posts on an annual basis.

10. The State Department must work with Congress to restore the Capital Security Cost Sharing Program [for embassy construction] at its full capacity, adjusted for inflation to approximately $2.2 billion in fiscal year 2015.

- The FY14 President's Budget included a request for $2.2 billion in the Embassy Security, Construction, and Maintenance account.

- The just-filed Omnibus Appropriations bill includes $2.4 billion for this account in regular and Overseas Contingency Operations funding.

11. The Board supports the State Department's initiative to request additional Marines and expand the Marine Security Guard (MSG) Program – as well as corresponding requirements for staffing and funding.

- Working with the Department of Defense, we are accelerating the deployment of 35 new Marine Security Guard detachments to U.S. diplomatic facilities. Eight detachments are already in place. Fourteen new detachments are expected to be in place by the end of 2014 and we will continue to work with the Department of Defense to deploy the remaining thirteen detachments. Additionally, MSG staffing has been increased at 16 high threat/high risk posts to a minimum level of 13 Marines (1 Detachment Commander and 12 Marine Security Guards).Working with Congress, the Department has requested and received more resources to build facilities at additional posts to host Marine Security Guards in the future.

- The Marine Corps also established the Marine Security Augmentation Unit in Quantico, Virginia, which will be able to provide MSGs on short notice at the request of Chiefs of Mission. These Marines are drawn from combat units, and have extra training in close-quarters battle, trauma, and weapons and tactics. Nine squads will be available by the end of January 2014.

STAFFING HIGH RISK, HIGH THREAT POSTS

12. The Board strongly endorses the Department's request for increased DS personnel for high- and critical-threat posts and for additional Mobile Security Deployment teams, as well as an increase in DS domestic staffing in support of such action.

- With Congressional support, the Department created 151 new Diplomatic Security positions. 113 employees, including 75 new DS agents, were hired in 2013. The remaining 38 employees will be hired in FY 2014.

13. The Department should assign key policy, program, and security personnel at high risk, high threat posts for a minimum of one year. For less critical personnel, the temporary duty length (TDY) length should be no less than 120 days.

- All high threat posts now have a minimum of a one-year tour of duty. We ensure overlap between incumbent and incoming positions to facilitate continuity of operations at high threat posts.

- Temporary duty assignments at high-threat posts are set at a minimum of 120 days.

14. The Department needs to review the staffing footprints at high risk, high threat posts, with particular attention to ensuring adequate Locally Employed Staff (LES) and management support. High risk, high threat posts must be funded and the human resources process prioritized to hire Locally Employed Staff interpreters and translators.

- The Department surveyed every post to review staffing numbers of (including LES interpreters and translators) on staff, and found that there was adequate staffing.

15. With increased and more complex diplomatic activities in the Middle East, the Department should enhance its ongoing efforts to significantly upgrade its language capacity, especially Arabic, among American employees, including DS, and receive greater resources to do so.

- The Department is ramping up the language capacity of its American employees, including Diplomatic Security agents, especially in Arabic. Increasing language capacity takes time – certain languages take up to 2 years to learn to the required level of proficiency. In the short term, the Department is committed to better equipping the growing cadre of security experts to engage local populations and cooperate with host nation security forces.

- The first offering of an intensive, 10-week "Arabic Alert" language course specifically for security personnel took place from October-December 2013. We are currently assessing the results of the course and making adjustments as needed.

TRAINING AND AWARENESS

16. A panel of Senior Special Agents and Supervisory Special Agents should revisit DS high-threat training with respect to active internal defense and fire survival as well as Chief of Mission (COM) protective detail training.

- The Department established a panel of Supervisory Special Agents to participate in a Program Review of the High Threat Tactical Course; as a result, DS revised high-threat training and COM protective detail training and raised standards for passing the High Threat Tactical Course.

- The panel's findings resulted in the identification and development of 170 operational requirements, associated proficiency standards, and training plans needed by DS special agents operating in high-threat, high risk environments. These findings were codified into a new High Threat Training Strategy that encompasses a career-long cycle of instruction for all DS special agents and includes new training courses for entry-, mid-, and senior-level agents.

17. The Diplomatic Security Training Center and Foreign Service Institute should collaborate in designing joint courses that integrate high threat training and risk management decision processes for senior and mid-level DS agents and Foreign Service Officers and better prepare them for leadership positions in high risk, high threat posts.

- The Department has enhanced security training efforts, including by requiring personnel headed to high threat posts to receive additional, specialized security and fire survival training.

- The Diplomatic Security Training Center and Foreign Service Institute have formed a working group to coordinate collaboration efforts on high-threat training and risk management, including the development of new courses and integration of updated course materials in a broad range of existing training.

SECURITY AND FIRE SAFETY EQUIPMENT

18. The Department should ensure provision of adequate fire safety and security equipment for safe havens and safe areas in non-Inman/SECCA facilities, as well as high threat Inman facilities.

- The Department has surveyed fire and life safety equipment requirements at all high-threat, high-risk U.S. diplomatic posts abroad. The Department has ensured that all high-threat, high-risk posts have adequate fire safety equipment; we installed new photo luminescent tape in safe havens; and have procured additional personal protective equipment.

- We were able to do this with the Increased Security Proposal money funded by Congress in FY 2013, for which we are grateful.

19. There have been technological advancements in non-lethal deterrents, and the State Department should ensure it rapidly and routinely identifies and procures additional options for non-lethal deterrents in high risk, high threat posts and trains personnel on their use.

- The Department has addressed this recommendation.

20. DS should upgrade surveillance cameras at high risk, high threat posts for greater resolution, nighttime visibility, and monitoring capability beyond post.

- Over the next year the Department will have upgraded all high-threat, high-risk facilities with more modern surveillance cameras.

- Equipment to support these cameras has already been procured and installed at 90 percent of our high-threat, high-risk posts.

INTELLIGENCE AND THREAT ANALYSIS

21. Careful attention should be given to factors showing a deteriorating threat situation in general as a basis for improving security posture. Key trends must be quickly identified and used to sharpen risk calculations.

- The Department has addressed this recommendation.

22. The DS Office of Intelligence and Threat Analysis should report directly to the DS Assistant Secretary and directly supply threat analysis to all DS components, regional Assistant Secretaries, and Chiefs of Mission in order to get key security-related threat information into the right hands more rapidly.

- The DS Office of Intelligence and Threat Analysis, now reports directly to the Assistant Secretary for Diplomatic Security for threat reporting and supplies threat analysis to regional Assistant Secretaries and Chiefs of Mission.

PERSONNEL ACCOUNTABILITY

23. The Board is of the view that findings of unsatisfactory leadership performance by senior officials in relation to the security incident under review should be a potential basis for discipline recommendations by future ARBs, and would recommend a revision of Department regulations or amendment to the relevant statute to this end.

- The Department is working with Congress to increase accountability. In January 2013, the Department proposed legislation to grant future Accountability Review Boards the authority to recommend disciplinary action on the basis of unsatisfactory leadership, and thus increase accountability for security incidents.

24. The Board was humbled by the courage and integrity shown by those on the ground in Benghazi and Tripoli, in particular the DS agents and Annex team who defended their colleagues… We trust that the Department and relevant agencies will take the opportunity to recognize their exceptional valor and performance, which epitomized the highest ideals of government service.

- The President and the Secretary of State have publicly mentioned the bravery and heroic efforts of our personnel on numerous occasions.

- The Department bestowed the Holbrooke award on Ambassador Chris Stevens; the Thomas Jefferson award to the personnel who gave their lives in September; the Secretary's award to one officer who was seriously injured; and the Secretary's Heroism Award to 12 personnel who defended the Benghazi facilities.

Appendix B. Selected Congressional Hearings on Benghazi Attack

Hearing Title	Committee	Date
Defense Department's posture for September 11, 2013: What are the Lessons of Benghazi?	House Armed Services Committee, Subcommittee on Oversight and Investigations	September 19, 2013
Reviews of the Benghazi Attack and Unanswered Questions	House Oversight and Government Reform Committee	September 19, 2013
Benghazi: Where is the State Department Accountability?	House Foreign Affairs Committee	September 18, 2013
S. 980, "Chris Stevens, Sean Smith, Tyrone Woods and Glen Doherty Embassy Security and Personnel Protection Act of 2013" *(Hearing and markup)*	Senate Foreign Relations Committee	July 16, 2013
Benghazi: Exposing Failure and Recognizing Courage	House Oversight and Government Reform Committee	May 8, 2013
Attack on U.S. Facilities in Benghazi, Libya	Senate Armed Services Committee	February 7, 2013
Terrorist Attack in Benghazi: The Secretary of State's View	House Foreign Affairs Committee	January 23, 2013
Benghazi: The Attacks and the Lessons Learned	Senate Foreign Relations Committee	January 23, 2013
Benghazi and Beyond: What Went Wrong on September 11, 2012 and How to Prevent it from Happening at other Frontline Posts (Part II)	House Foreign Affairs Committee	December 20, 2012
Benghazi: The Attack and the Lessons Learned	Senate Foreign Relations Committee	December 20, 2012
Closed hearing on the circumstances, including the intelligence and security situation, surrounding the recent terrorist attack in Benghazi, Libya	Senate Select Intelligence Committee	November 16, 2012
Benghazi and Beyond: What Went Wrong on September 11, 2012 and How to Prevent it from Happening at other Frontline Posts (Part I)	House Foreign Affairs Committee	November 15, 2012
Closed oversight hearing on the circumstances, including the intelligence and security situation, surrounding the recent terrorist attack in Benghazi, Libya, and the intelligence and security situation in other Arab Spring countries	Senate Select Intelligence Committee	November 15, 2012
The Security Failures of Benghazi	House Oversight and Government Reform Committee	October 10, 2012

Source: CRS. See respective committee websites for witness lists and testimony.

Note: Includes only hearings in which the Benghazi attack was the main subject.

Appendix C. Selected Diplomatic Security-Related Legislation, 112th and 113th Congresses (in Chronological Order)

Measure (and date introduced)	Title	Summary
H.Res. 36 (introduced 1/18/2013)	Establishing a select committee to investigate and report on the attack on the United States consulate in Benghazi, Libya	Establishes a select committee to investigate and report on the attack on the United States consulate in Benghazi, Libya
S. 227 (introduced 2/4/2013)	Embassy Security Funds Transfer Act of 2013	Authorizes funds appropriated under the Department of State, Foreign Operations, and Related Programs Appropriations Act of 2012 under the headings "Diplomatic and Consular Programs" and "Embassy Security, Construction, and Maintenance" to be transferred between such headings
H.R. 731 (introduced 2/14/2013)	Protecting Americans Abroad Act	Authorizes the State Department to use to the "Best-Value Contracting" award method for local guard forces in high-risk areas when deemed necessary
H.R. 925 (introduced 2/28/2013)	Securing Accountability in Foreign Embassies (SAFE Embassies) Act	Amends the Diplomatic Security Act to require a determination by the Accountability Review Board that an individual's misconduct or unsatisfactory performance of duty significantly contributed to serious injury, loss of life, significant property destruction, or serious security breach in order for the Board to recommend that an investigatory or disciplinary action be initiated by the appropriate federal agency or instrumentality
P.L. 113-6, §1708 (introduced 3/4/2013)	FY2013 Consolidated and Further Continuing Appropriations Act, 2013	Congress provided the Department of State with the authority to transfer more than $1 billion from Iraq Operations OCO funds to accounts addressing global security needs, as requested in State's Increased Security Proposal.

Measure (and date introduced)	Title	Summary
H.R. 1186 (introduced 3/14/2013)	To posthumously award the Congressional Gold Medal to each of Glen Doherty and Tyrone Woods in recognition of their contributions to the Nation.	Directs the Speaker of the House of Representatives and the President pro tempore of the Senate to arrange for the posthumous award, on behalf of Congress, of a gold medal in commemoration of the contributions of Glen Doherty and Tyrone Woods, two former Navy SEAL members who sacrificed their lives on September 11, 2012, while serving as part of a U.S. diplomatic security detachment in Libya
H.R. 1768 (introduced 4/26/2013)	Accountability Review Board Reform Act of 2013	Amends the Diplomatic Security Act to improve the effectiveness of ARBs by increasing their independence from the State Department through, among other measures, changing the composition of the membership of ARBs to have fewer State-appointed members, and specifying conflict of interest guidelines
H.R. 1781 (introduced 4/26/2013)	Mustafa Akarsu Local Guard Force Support Act	Seeks to assist the family members of Foreign Service Nationals (FSN) killed in the line of duty by making them eligible to obtain special visas to immigrate to the United States
H.R. 2723 (introduced 7/18/2013)	Embassy Security and Enhancement Act of 2013	Enhances security for facilities and personnel at United States diplomatic and consular posts abroad through improved training, procedures, and resources
S. 1372 (see also S.Rept. 113-81) (introduced 7/25/2013)	Department of State, Foreign Operations, and Related Programs Appropriations Act, Fiscal Year 2014	Recommends appropriation levels for diplomatic security-related spending
H.R. 2855 (see also H.Rept. 113-185) (introduced 7/30/2013)	Making appropriations for the Department of State, foreign operations, and related programs for the fiscal year ending September 30, 2014, and for other purposes	Recommends appropriation levels for diplomatic security-related spending
H.R. 3547 / P.L. 113-76 (introduced 11/20/2013)	Consolidated Appropriations Act, 2014	Fully funds Administration's FY2014 request on embassy security funding; provides $2.674 billion for Embassy Security, Construction and Maintenance account and $2.77 billion for Worldwide Security Protection.

Source: CRS.

Notes: Does not include legislative proposals pertaining to other agencies, such as the FY2014 National Defense Authorization Act and its provisions relating to the Marine Security Guard program.

Author Contact Information

Alex Tiersky
Analyst in Foreign Affairs
atiersky@crs.loc.gov, 7-7367

Key Policy Staff

Area of Expertise	Name	Phone	E-mail
Diplomatic Security Funding	Susan Epstein	7-7367	sepstein@crs.loc.gov
Libya	Christopher Blanchard	7-0428	cblanchard@crs.loc.gov
U.S. Marine Corps	Andrew Feickert	7-7673	afeickert@crs.loc.gov

www.ingramcontent.com/pod-product-compliance
Lightning Source LLC
Chambersburg PA
CBHW080807290526

45790CB00008B/3609